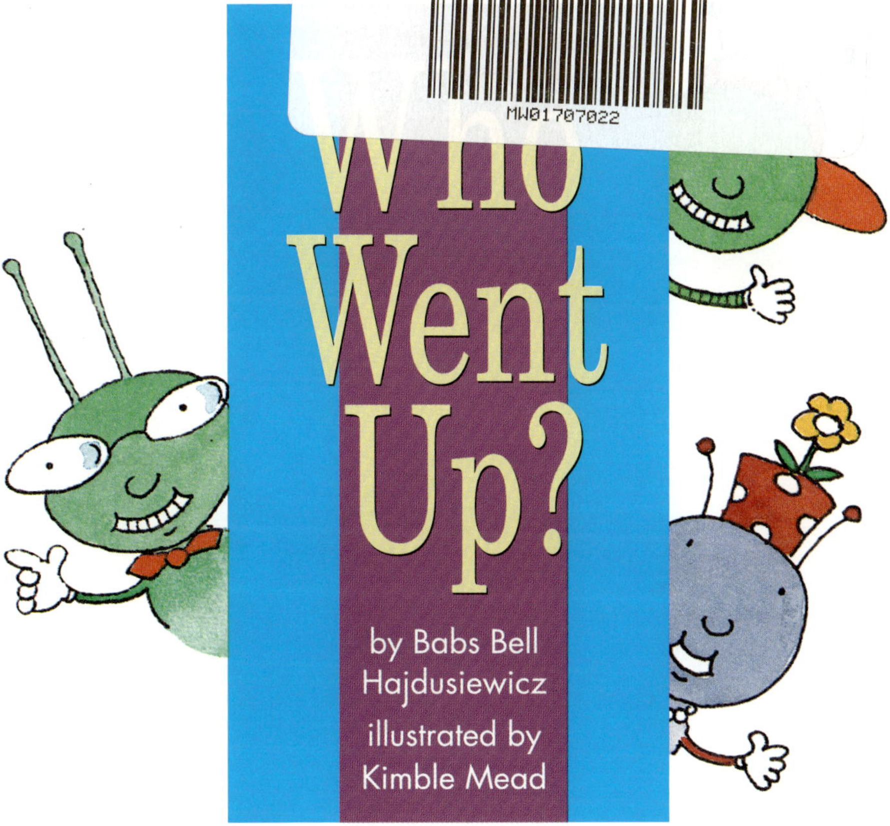

MODERN CURRICULUM PRESS
Pearson Learning Group

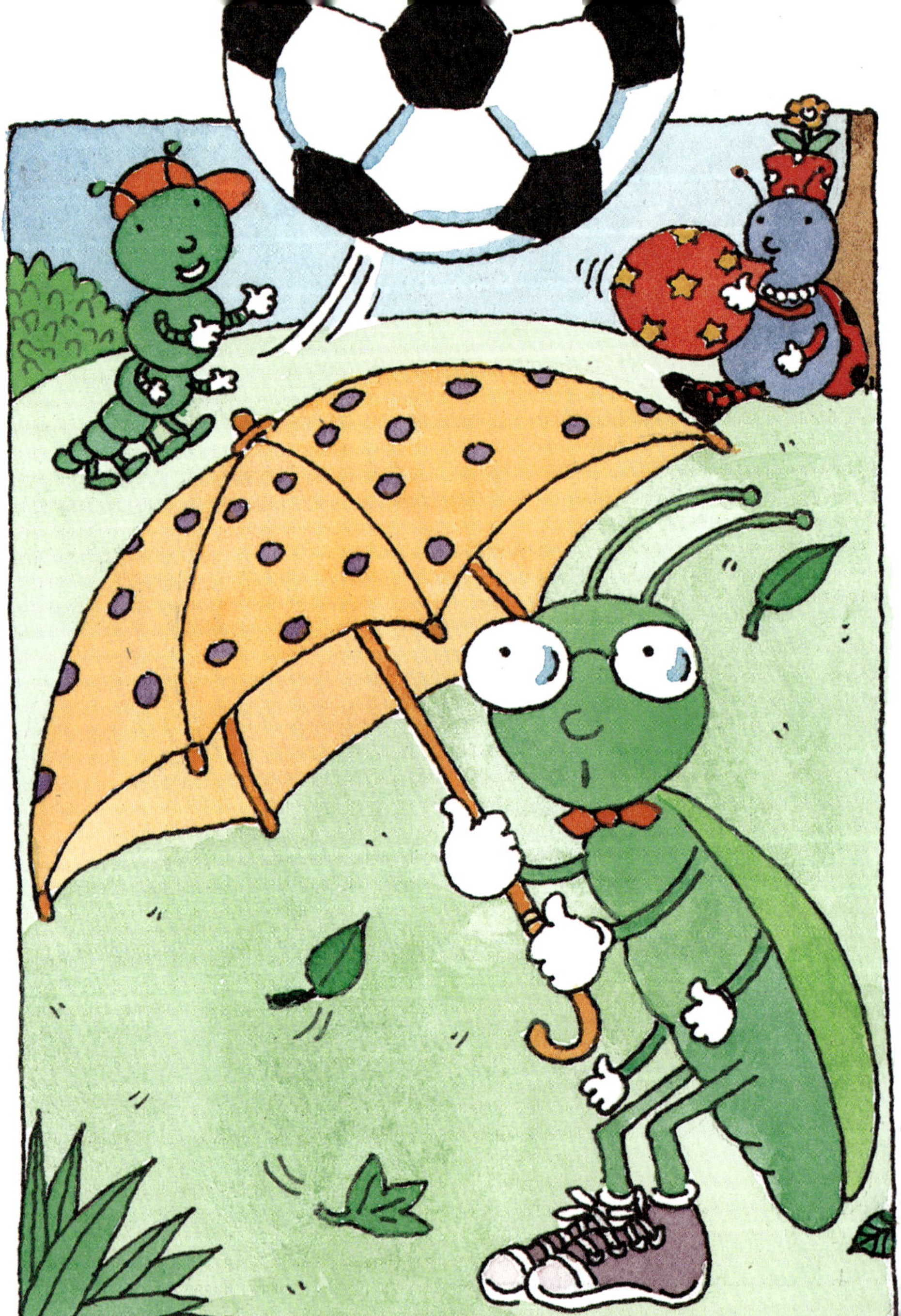

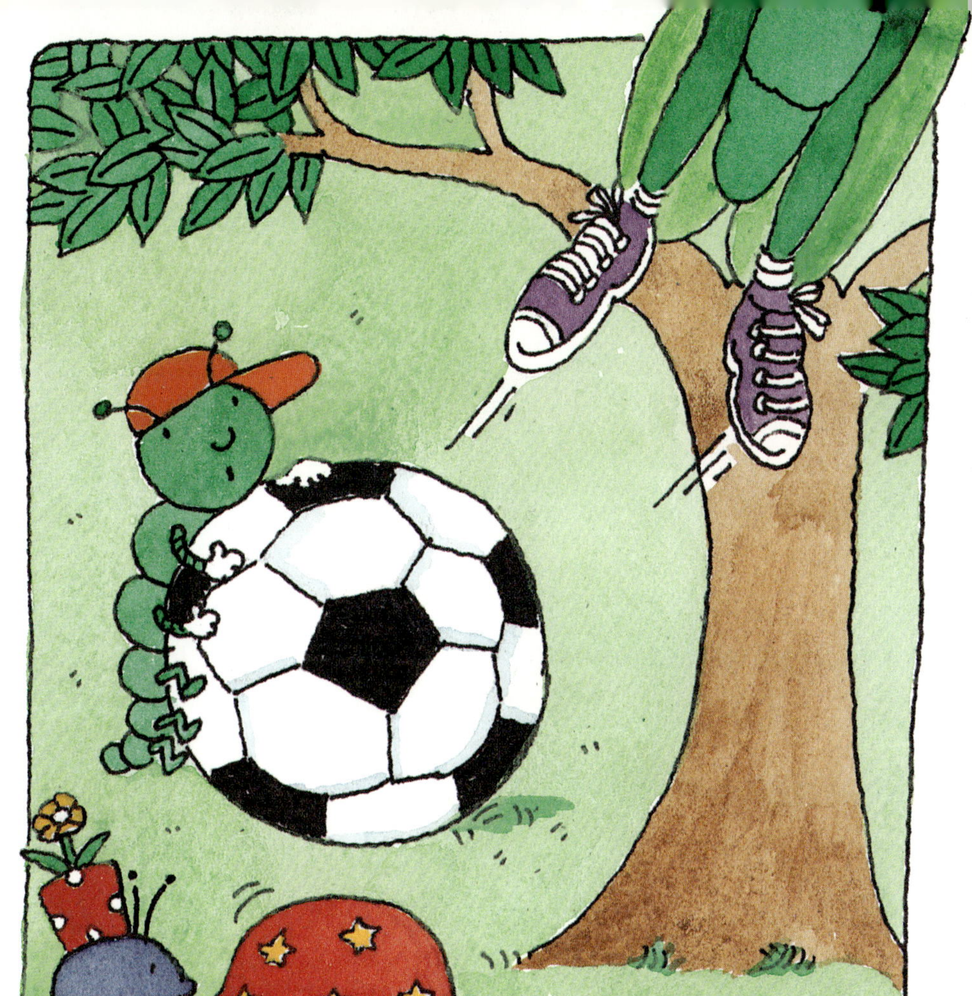

Who went up?

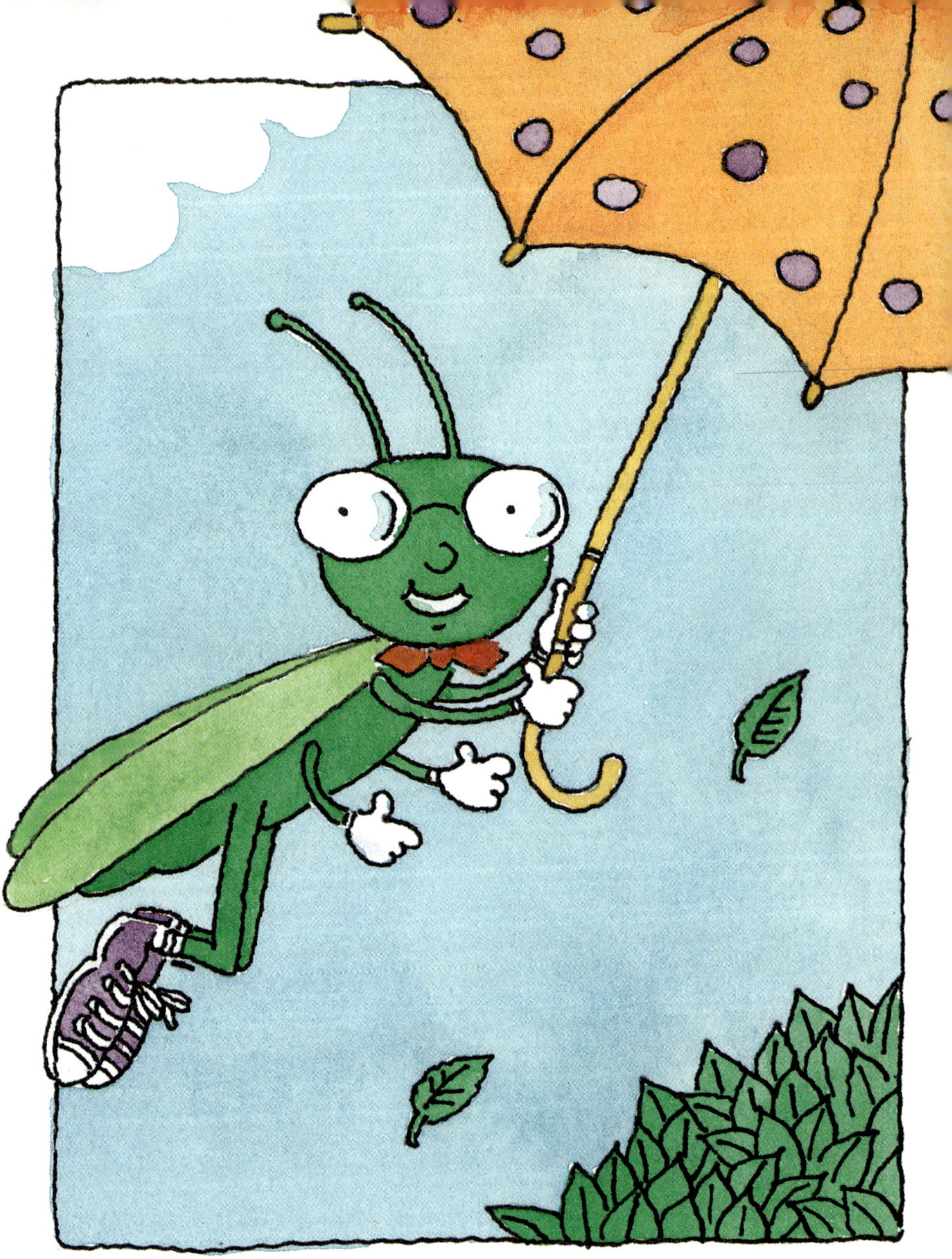

I did!

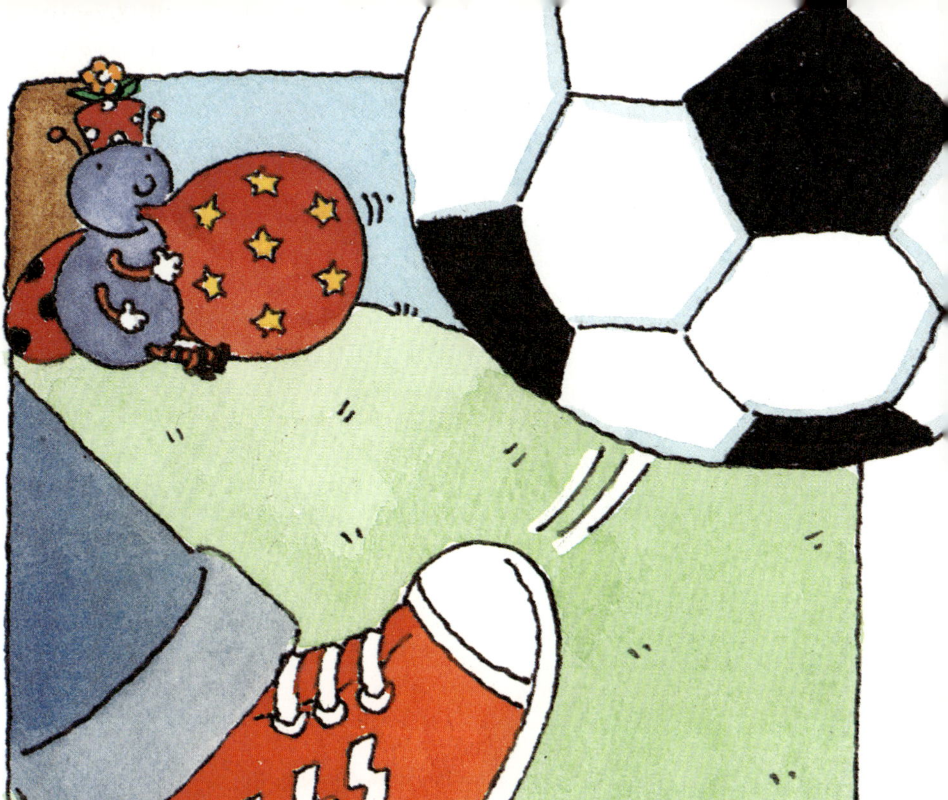

Who went up?

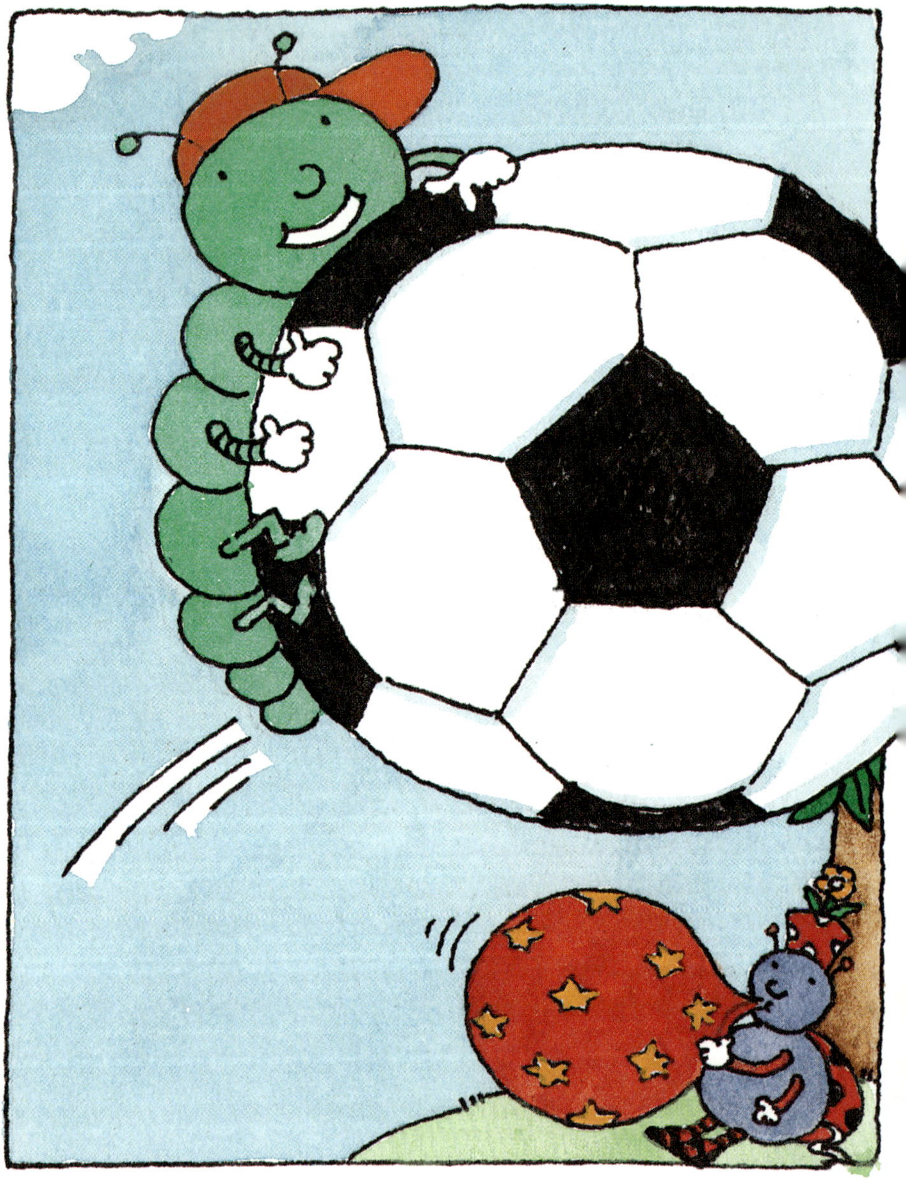

I did!

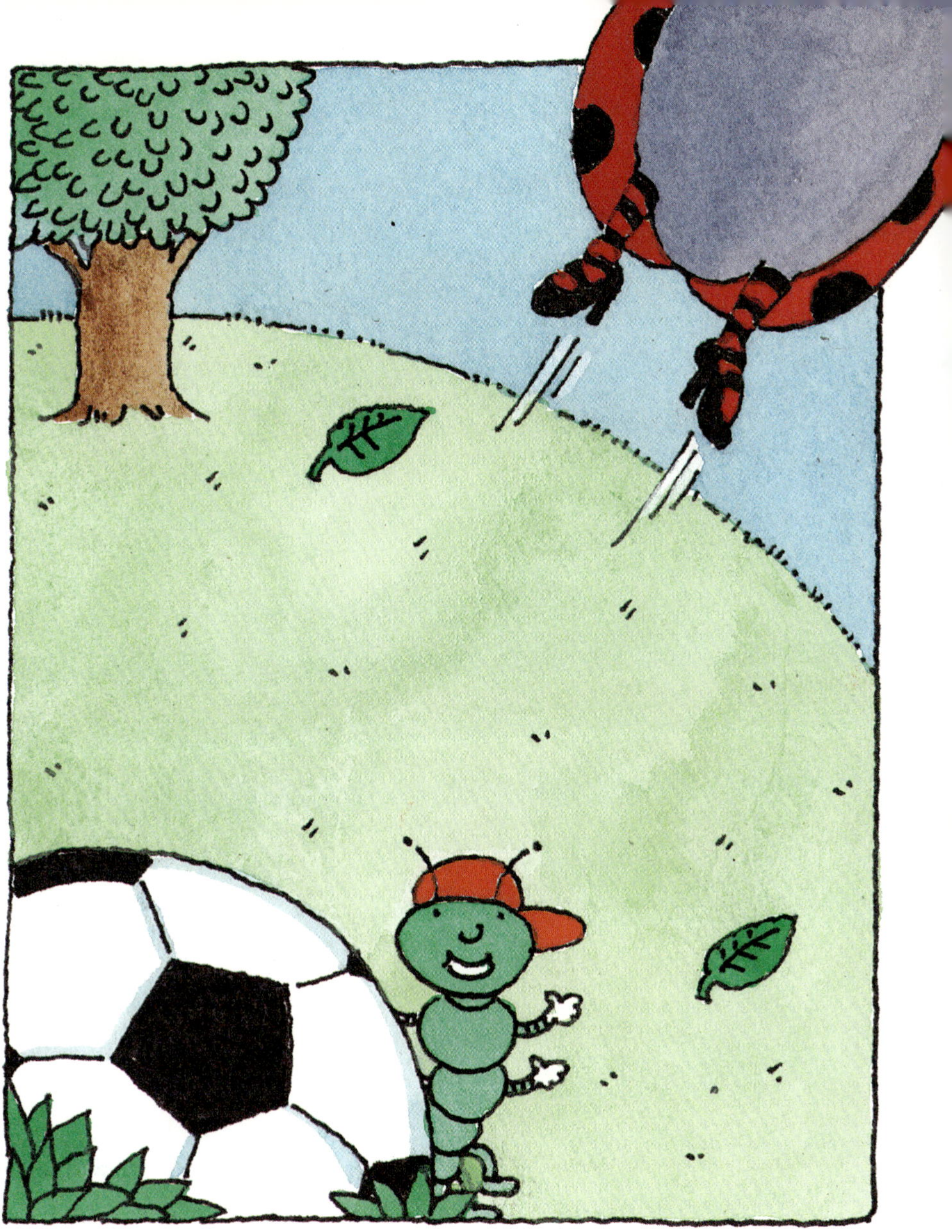

Who went up?

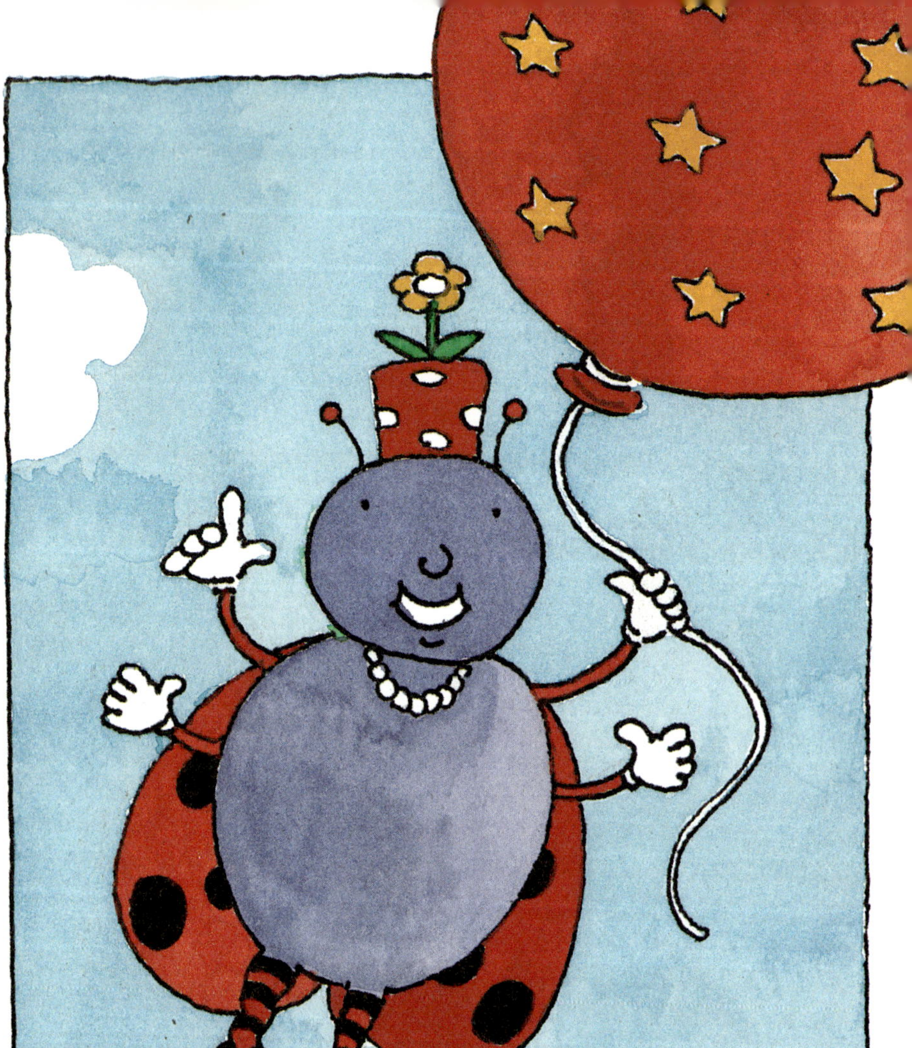

I did!

Look at me!